THE
OTHER SIDE OF THE SUN

DOLLY BAKER

ARCHWAY
PUBLISHING

Archway Publishing books may be ordered through booksellers or by contacting:

Archway Publishing
1663 Liberty Drive
Bloomington, IN 47403
www.archwaypublishing.com
844-669-3957

ISBN: 978-1-6657-3313-7 (sc)
ISBN: 978-1-6657-3312-0 (e)

Library of Congress Control Number: 2022920807

Print information available on the last page.

Archway Publishing rev. date: 12/8/2022

INTRODUCTION

It was the blue lights for me! As soon as the blue lights hit my rear view mirror, fear took over. *Shit! Not again! Maybe I can get by this time.* The problem was I knew I had been drinking. As the officer approached my vehicle, I felt my body going into shock.

"License and registration. Do you know why I pulled you over?"

Actually, I did not know why I had been pulled over, but I tried my best to comply and hold in the anger that was boiling inside of me.

"No sir, I do not," I stated honestly.

"You were speeding. I clocked you at 49 in a 35 mile zone," the officer stated. "Have you been drinking?"

"Yes, earlier I had a couple shots but they should be worn off by now." I was lying through my teeth, but anything to get out of getting another DUI. I actually had more than just a couple of shots; I had a little bit of beer and smoked some weed, which for me is a bad combination.

"I am going to do a sobriety test on you."

That is where my story ended or began, whichever way you take this story. I had received a DUI eleven years prior and I could not believe I got myself in this situation again. As a matter of fact, I should not have been so surprised. Over the course of the eleven years, I was still drinking and driving. I just never got caught. I would go on to take the officer on a spiral of my aggressive rage that could have landed me in jail if he wanted to be an asshole about it. He was rather calm, sending smart remarks back at me but nonetheless, he held his composure much better than I could.

This time was different. When I received my first DUI, I was eighteen years old with no real plans for life. I was just out there having fun and doing what I wanted to do. The second time, I had three children who depended solely on me to care for them. I felt like I had failed them. I often did things without regard to how it could affect those around me. One thing about it: whenever I did not live righteously, life had a way of catching up with me.

What is the righteous way to live anyway? I never really knew, and by then I should have figured it out. I would go on to be sentenced to five days in jail. I had never been to jail before. The first time I was caught, I only stayed for two hours. Being locked down for twenty-four hours a day, I had nothing but time to think—a lot. The problem resting in my mind was the fact that I was supposed to have stopped drinking months before. I was addicted to the numbing of the pain that alcohol did for me—at least that is what I thought it was doing. Drinking did nothing more than cause me more problems, and I had finally reached my breaking point. I never thought I was addicted to alcohol, but alcohol was my go-to for whenever I found myself in an emotional state. I do not know how it became an addiction, but I knew from that point on that it had to end—now!

ONE

When a child does not know who he or she is, the child is bound to create an identity based off what he or she sees from the adults in his or her life.

I was born in 1992 in Jamaica, Queens, New York. Of course, I do not remember too much of the first three years of my childhood, but I would like to believe my mother cared for me to the best of her ability.

In August of 1995, my two older sisters and I were getting on a plane with a social worker to head to Kentucky. I was told as a child that my grandmother (my mother's mother) had passed away, and my sisters and I were adopted by my middle sister's biological grandmother on her father's side. That right there says a lot. How could all three of my mother's children have to be adopted by someone else while she was still living? She did not pass away until six years later, while I was in fourth grade. She was a phone call mom. She called just about every day to ask about school and to make sure I was being a good girl and brushing my teeth—you know, all the things a mother would know if she were actually raising her children. To me, that was enough. I felt loved by her. I really believed she cared. But I would grow up later to resent her for not physically being present. That was not the worse part though. The most painful experiences I encountered happened when she was not around.

The absence of a mother's love is the absence of the heart in a child. My mother birthed a heartless being who was good at pretending to love with no clear example of how and whom to love, especially myself.

My sisters never liked me. Regardless of what they might say, actions speak louder than words. Their actions were extremely loud. When we first moved to Kentucky, we all slept in one big bed. Of course, as the youngest and the smallest, I had to sleep in the middle. I hated sharing a bed with them because all night I would hear, "Get off of me!" or "Move over!" or "Do not touch me!" I was given no room in the bed to maneuver at all. I would attempt to lay face up and be as still as possible. My grandma had a three bedroom, two-and-a-half bathroom house. One of the bedrooms was a study. Eventually, the study became the bedroom of my oldest sister, Iris; my middle sister Aster and I shared a room. I would sometimes sleep in the bed with my grandma to avoid hearing my sister complain.

Iris was usually assigned to do my hair. Sometimes she would braid it so tight it would be hard to sleep because my eyes felt like they were being pried open. One time, as she was doing my hair, I was writing in my journal. I wrote in my journal that I wanted to know who my father was. The next day I planned on asking Mommy. Iris was reading over my shoulder.

"Aww, Essence wants to know who her daddy is! There is no need to ask Mommy. That's dumb to ask," she exclaimed.

I kind of felt stupid for writing it, but also embarrassed by her reading my most private journal entry. My sisters made it well known by their various bullying tactics that my feelings were not important. They knew most of my fears and used them against me in torturous ways. Our neighbor had this big dog named Spider. I was terrified of Spider because I was not tall and he stood taller than me—at least it seemed like he did. One morning, Grandma (she was my adopted mother, but I called her Grandma due to her old age) had left early to go to the doctor, I believe. She left well before school. We had to put ourselves on the bus at the driveway next door. My sisters knew the night before that Spider had gotten loose from his chain and was somewhere wandering around. I was so afraid to walk outside, but I felt a bit of relief knowing they would be walking with me—or so I thought. They told me I had to walk to the bus stop by myself. I was so afraid to see Spider. I just knew he would try to jump on me or bite me, and I did not want that to happen. I begged and pleaded with them to walk with me to the bus stop, but they refused. I did not understand. We were all getting on the same bus. Why did I have to walk by myself? I cried for Grandma.

"Grandma cannot come save you now. Get to the bus stop and hurry up." They laughed.

I cried for Mommy. Well that was stupid of me. She was thousands of miles away. What could she have done to save me?

"Girl, you so stupid for crying for Mommy, really! How can she help you? Grandma said you had to walk to the bus stop by yourself or you are going to get in trouble." They laughed some more.

I never understood how my fears could bring them enjoyment. I felt like I was going to dammit piss on myself. I slowly started walking to the bus stop, constantly looking back to see if they were following. I often wonder if Spider had attacked me, would they have even helped. They probably would have loved to see my face chewed off and my body left for dead.

When they were not finding ways to disturb my peace, they were fighting each other. As much as I disliked them at the moment, I did not like to see them fight each other either. One morning, they got into a big fight on the first day of school. I cannot lie; it was quite funny watching them pull each other's hair and claw at each other's faces. All Grandma knew was they had better not miss the school bus. I stood there just watching them tear into each other's bodies like they were strangers. Then this sad feeling came over me, and I wanted them to stop. I started crying, begging Grandma to make them stop. I could not watch it anymore, but Grandma just stood there and let them fight. I guess she figured eventually one of them was going to tire out. When I say these girls were clawing each other's skin, hunny, they looked like animals when it was all over. Grandma sent them to school looking how they were looking too.

They really hated that I was an honor-roll student and that I was often praised for being smart. I really was not that smart. I just felt like I was winging it. I winged it enough to get by. They fought me a lot, and shoved me against walls. I was a big ole crybaby. I often cried to Grandma every time they did something mean. Then they would be even meaner the next time because Grandma would fuss and tell them to leave me alone. They did not listen. I was the true definition of a *little sister*. No matter how mean they were, I still looked up to them and loved them dearly—maybe too much.

When I was young, I created a fantasy life to escape my reality. In my fantasy, I was being raised by loving parents. I had protective and loving siblings. I would tell myself every day that the life I was living was only temporary, and very soon my mother and father were coming to rescue me. I always had to wake up.

It was Christmas Day. I was eight years old. I could not wait to wake up and open my

Christmas presents. I learned early on that Santa was not real because Grandma would have us write lists for Santa, and then take us to the store and tell us to pick out the items on our lists. I did not care if he was real or not. I just enjoyed the gifts. When I woke up, only one of my sisters was at the house. Iris was not there. I wondered why. While opening gifts, my grandma was on the phone discussing something very serious with someone. After she got off the phone, she stated that she was going to pick up Iris. I asked to ride along.

We pulled onto this long path, and in the distance I could see a trailer and a police officer pulling in right in front of us. Iris had a habit of stealing any bicycle she could get her hands on to run away to her boyfriend's house. This time Grandma called the police to go with us to pick her up—on Christmas Day! That did not stop her. She ran away quite often. Eventually, she was sent to a girls' group home in Missouri, and later back to New York. Before her relocation, an incident took places that forever lives on in my mind.

At Grandma's house, there was a lot of yard and a lot of land. Also located in the area were my aunt's house and my aunt's in-law's house. Behind my aunt's house was a basketball court where the neighborhood children and families would come together to play. On this day, my grandma's sister was visiting from out of town. All the kids were outside in the yard or on the basketball court, or so we thought. It started to get dark, and it was time to head home. No one was at my grandma's house while we were outside playing. When we got home, we found that the storm door in the front of the house had been broken. It was as if a big rock was thrown into it. Of course, I did not know what happened. My grandma asked all of us if we came to the house while she was not there. Iris stated she believed one of the boys from the neighborhood may have thrown the rock through the glass. Grandma was not having it. She blamed her for breaking the glass on the storm door. An argument about the door took place and, before I knew it, Grandma had Iris's head pinned to the top of our couch and was punching her repeatedly in the face. One thing about Grandma was that she wore a lot of jewelry, which included a lot of rings on her hand. It was painful and horrible to watch. My grandma's sister and her husband tried to make her stop, but I could see the rage in Grandma's eyes. She was not going to let up. I began to cry, began pleading for grandma to stop, and eventually she did. I never found out who broke the storm door glass, but I knew one thing for certain: Iris had to suffer for it.

I caught on early that my siblings and I were just an extra source of income for Grandma. We came with paychecks to front the bills every month. I later in life found out that my oldest sister's check was not coming to the home, and one who does not contribute, whether voluntarily or involuntarily, is an extra mouth and a burden. It was easy for Grandma to get rid of her. So much for keeping my siblings and me together.

Not too long after, I remember Iris not being in the home with us anymore. When she went to the group home, she wrote me letters and sent pictures. Though she was just as mean as Aster, I would have preferred for to have stayed and Aster to have been the one to leave. She was the meanest. I had an aunt in New York who took Iris in. At the time, my mother was still living and Iris was able to see her more often than I did. I am pretty sure my mother did not attempt to get off drugs to be the best mother she could be. I always dreamed of the day my mother would get sober and come back into my life full time. That dream was very short-lived by the fall of 2001.

TWO

I always loved school. School was where I got a break from home. With Iris gone, that left Aster in the house to wreak havoc on my life. As stated before, she was the meanest one of them. I used to wonder why she hated me as much as she did. I would often encounter people who would give me money. After church was my favorite time. I knew I would get at least a couple of dollars to be able to go to the nearby gas station and but my own candy before going home.

I would often ask Aster if we could go to the movies together or hang out but she would state she did not have time for me. Most of her time was spent in her bedroom by herself; other days she would stay away, I guess hanging out with her friends. Who would want to spend time with a little kid when they were teenagers, sister or not? It would have been nice to have some type of bond. She was not the bonding type, and as the years went by I came to realize that she did not love anyone but herself. I slowly started giving up the idea of us ever having a real sister-bond-type-relationship and I gravitated more towards having friends. My friends would become my family.

I had a cousin Lily; she was not really my cousin, but that is what we always called each other, even to this day. She lived in North Carolina and would come visit her grandma during the summers and holidays. Her grandma lived in the same neighborhood as I did. I loved when Lily came for the summer because I would have someone to play with and would not have to sit in the house with mean ole Aster. As I got older, I caught on that this Lily's grandma did not like me. Lily was not allowed to come to my grandma's house, so we would meet at the ditch. The ditch is a nigga-rigged drain between my grandma's house and everyone else's. Her grandma did not like her playing with me and she always told her not to call me her cousin. Well, I knew early on who my biological family was and who was not, so I did not see why it was such a problem what we called each other. To make it extra bad, her grandma was a minister. Not everyone who preaches about "love thy neighbor" lives by those words. My cousin did not treat me differently. She was my cousin and I was hers and that was all we knew. We did go to school together in pre-kindergarten and kindergarten before she relocated to North Carolina.

One of the worst feelings in the world is to not only know but to feel that you are not wanted and the people you are around do not want you. This is especially true when there is absolutely nothing you can do about it besides pretend as if you are clueless to their actions. I wanted to run away so many times in my youth, but where was I going to go? My own mother did not want me. I could not expect anyone else to want to take me in.

I always admired Aster, even though she often neglected me. She was mean and I wanted to be mean just like her. She showed little to no emotion, and often times I believed that nothing or no one could hurt her feelings. I wanted to be just like that. I wanted to have the inability to be hurt by anything or anyone. I often received money from different people for being a cute little girl, or so they said. I loved going to church because after service I would make my rounds to collect my dollar bills. Before we got home, I would ask Grandma to stop at the gas station up the street from our house. The majority of the time, I would buy candy that was in wrappers. I liked to share. I did not have much to offer at that time, but I believed if I shared my candy with Aster then that would give her reason to be nice to me. When I believed she was mad at me because she had not spoken to me, I would take a few pieces of my candy and put it under her bedroom door. Then I would run back to my room and peek down the hall to see if she had picked it up. If she moved the candy that meant she loved me, but if she left it there she hated me. That was one of the ways I determined our relationship in my mind. If I did something for her, that gave her no choice but to love me because she would see how nice I was and how willing I was to do anything for her love.

I was a highly sensitive child. In my child-like mind, I always believed that one day my mother would come and rescue me. She just needed a break. I always felt out of place in my home. I had little to no affection from my sisters. There was constant fighting and arguing in my home and no place for me to escape. My sisters never tried to have a bond or even a relationship with me in my early childhood, and their ability to express their dislike for me was very apparent. I just wanted to be liked—no, loved by them, just like the families on television. I wanted a mother and a father with a happy family, but my family was far from happy. I never got to the root of the problem of the tension between my sisters and me. I just knew it hurt to desire love that they would never give.

I do not quite remember when I found out my mother was on drugs and my dream of us becoming a family would never come true. One day, I just knew. I saw an episode of MTV *Cribs* one day, and the show was about Usher Raymond. He showed his big, beautiful house in Atlanta, Georgia. My favorite part of his home was the section he had for his mother. It was like a whole other house inside of his house just for her. I dreamed of growing up and moving to Atlanta, buying a big house, and putting a section in my house just for my mother. I would help her get off drugs and better her life. I knew if she would never be a good mother to me, she could at least be a great grandmother. I was going to have my happy and loving family one way or another—until one fall day in fourth grade when I came home and had to reevaluate my dreams once again.

Mommy called just about every evening after school to check on us. This particular night, I had already spoken with her but the thought had come in my mind to ask her who my father was. I had to wait until the next day for her to call so I just wrote it in my journal how excited I was for the next day to come. I thought about this unknown man often. Even if we could never meet, I would have liked to at least know what he looked like. Did I look like him? Was he tall or short? Did he have other children? Maybe I would have some nicer siblings on his side. I wanted to know everything and Mommy was going to tell me. I could not get off the bus fast enough. I ran to the door excited because I was going to be able to talk to Mommy and ask about my father. I came in the house and kissed Grandma, took my coat and shoes off, and proceeded to remove the items from my book bag. Aster went to her room. I was listening, waiting in anticipation for the phone to ring. When it finally did, I could feel the excitement rising in my body. It was as if I was finally going to solve a mystery. I could hear Grandma on the phone, but her voice did not sound too pleasant. "Oh no, oh no, when did this happen? Okay, I will tell them." Grandma sounded so sad. I came out of my room believing maybe Mommy had not called yet. Aster was right behind me coming out of her room after hearing the same sad tone of Grandma's voice.

"What happened?" asked Aster, with the same sense of worry as me.

"I do not know. I think your daddy died," I foolishly responded. I do not know why that was the first thing to come to my mind when she asked, but it just made sense. We both knew someone had possibly passed away, but I was not prepared for what I was to hear next.

"It is your mom; she did not wake up this morning. They believed she had a heart attack," said Grandma regretfully.

If Mommy had a heart attack, that meant she smoked enough crack and God knows what else to stop her heart. I longed to be more important in her life than drugs were, but the truth of the matter was that I was not. Grandma did not tell me when I was a kid that Mommy was a crackhead and I wish she had. It would have been better to know that the dream I had of saving Mommy could never have come true. She did not want to be saved and she did not want to be a mother.

I instantly felt a feeling of regret. It was my fault—it had to be. It was as if someone was spinning me around and around quickly on this merry-go-round that I could not get off of. If I did not want to know who my father was, she would still be alive. She did not want me to love him—only her. Maybe he was not a good person and she feared if I found out about him he would hurt me. That must have been why she never told me previously. This was my fault. She knew—she knew—she had to know I was going to ask. I was just too nosy. I always had to know something, but it was not my business to know; because of my curiosity, Mommy did not wake up. She could not bear to tell me the truth. I broke my Mommy's heart. I killed her.

THREE

Pain, fear, abandonment, betrayal, confusion, hurt, remorse, sorrow, and anger—no, mostly anger is all I would feel for the next twenty years of my life. The distance between Aster and me grew. It got to the point that I slowly stopped caring about her. I did not care that I did not even know who she was.

I had a picture of Mommy in the door of the car that I traveled with the whole way to New York. I often just stared at the picture, feeling the most regret I had ever felt up until that point in my life. I was only nine years old. The dream I had of caring for my mother when I got older was crushed, and I did not know what I would do with my life anymore. Everyone else had a mommy. Why could I not have one? Iris was already living in New York again by the time Mommy died. I was excited to see her but not too excited—just happy, I guess.

The day of the funeral, we entered the funeral home and there were a few people I did not even know. I guessed some were her drug-addicted friends. How nice for them to come see her off. I sat at the casket just staring at her and trying to find the way to say I was sorry.

The pastor walked up to me and asked, "And what is your name pretty girl?"

"Essence," I stated while fighting back my tears.

He said some nice and comforting words, then he reached into his pocket and pulled out five dollars and handed it to me. I thanked him and turned around stare at Mommy. A little after the service began, it ended and it was time to leave. I felt as if I had not looked at Mommy long enough to remember her face. I needed to see her again; I just needed a few better looks before I never saw her face again. By that time, my aunt was pulling me towards the door as I tried to resist. I just had to see her one more time.

"Just let her go," Aster stated with the most irritation in her voice. I did not care though. I had to see Mommy, so I made up my mind that I would ignore her tone of rudeness. The last look I was able to get in was a quick glance as I was exiting the funeral home and that was it. No more seeing Mommy's face ever again. We got in the car to drive to the burial site. The car was rather quiet without the usual taunts I received from my siblings. Of course, I had to sit in the middle, but neither one of them wanted me touching them. I tried to make myself as small as possible so I would not touch them. I do not remember which one made the comment first, but the next thing I heard was probably the most ignorant comment to make on the occasion.

"All I am saying is we are her kids too. Why the pastor only gave you five dollars?"

"I did not get any money."

"What is so special about you?"

I sat there silently as they pushed and tried to keep me from touching them in the back of the car. I could not believe my ears. They were having a full-blown attitude over the pastor giving me five dollars that I did not even ask for in the first place. I wish I would have just ripped the five dollars in half and gave both of them a piece. I did not want the money. I did not care about the money. I wanted to cry. I wanted to feel compassion. It would have been nice if we could have been embracing each other like normal siblings do when a parent passes away. But we were far from normal—nowhere near normal.

I only had one solid memory of Mommy during our summer visits to New York. I had an aunt who lived in the projects. I later found out that she was not a blood aunt. My grandmother, who was my mother's mother, grew up in foster care and she had befriended a lady named Rose. They saw each other as sisters and that is how I came to have an aunt Rose. I loved Aunt Rose but I did not like going to her house. My Aunt Rose's house was where my Mommy would come and see my sisters and me. By this time, Iris was already living in New York again, so she saw Mommy regularly, and I would be able to see Iris as well. The projects stink. There was always a crackhead-looking person outside, and there were roaches—lots and lots of roaches. My favorite thing about going to Aunt Rose's house was the icees. She was the neighborhood icee lady. I would go with her as she sold icees to the people in the neighborhood. I especially liked the free icees I would receive.

This one particular day, we arrived at Aunt Rose's house and waited for Mommy to get there. When she came in, she had a bag full of goodies. Mommy always gave us clothes and other essentials that we needed such as toothbrushes, toothpaste, coffee, letters she had written, and things of that nature. Mommy was going through the bag of clothes and pulling out clothes that were obviously too big for me to wear. I did not complain; I just took the clothes and thanked her. I was happy just to receive something of sentiment from her. She pulled this jumpsuit out of the bag that was really big. Iris told her that it was too big for me to wear.

"This jumpsuit is not too big! I know what size my baby wear!" Mommy stated, apparently upset about the comment.

"No you do not know what size she wears! You can tell it is too big. Essence is not that big!" Iris yelled back at her.

They went back and forth for a while, arguing and yelling and arguing and yelling. All I could think was that it did not matter that it was too big—I could grow into it. I was just happy she gave me something. I wanted to cry so badly. I wanted them to stop arguing. I rarely saw Mommy and this was not how I wanted the encounter to go. Not too long afterward, she left Rose's house. I do not remember seeing her alive ever again.

A motherless child, especially a motherless girl, will never learn how to love herself. A mother is supposed to teach her daughter how to respect herself. I did not learn either one.

Months later during the school year, my grandma's sister, Aunt Daisy, came to visit. Aunt Daisy lived in Panama where my grandma was originally from. She did speak English but her accent was thick. One day, Grandma, Aunt Daisy, and I went grocery shopping. We came home, put the groceries away, and proceeded to have a regular night like any other night. I went to bed early because I had school the next day. When I woke the next morning, every light in the house seemed to be on and a foul smell was coming up the hall. I could hear my grandma crying and talking rather loudly. I went into Grandma's room to get ready for school as usual, but Grandma told me to leave the room. I glanced toward her bed and Aunt Daisy was sliding off the side of her bed with her eyes rolling in her head. She had urinated and released her bowels and was shaking in a seizure-like motion. I had never seen someone in the middle of dying before. I did not know what to do but I knew I wanted to help. Sometimes the best thing you can do in any given moment is exactly what you are told to do. I headed down the hall and got dressed for school. By the time the bus came, the ambulance and police officers were covering our front yard. I never saw Aunt Daisy alive again.

I was always an honor roll student and my sisters hated it. They mostly hated how much admiration I got from being an honor roll student, and that made me not like being smart. I never really thought I was smart anyway. I did not study. When I got home from school, I did not want to think about the schoolwork I had done that day, let alone homework. I just felt like I was average. I paid attention in class to the important stuff; on test days, I would sit in class trying to memorize everything that was going to be on the test. I read the study guides over and over until the tests were given. I learned early that Grandma did not like Ds and Fs. If I received a low grade on an assignment, I would just take the assignment out of the packet of assignments that Grandma had to sign off on each week. I would leave one or two assignments with a low grade to make it look realistic. I was an honor roll student, not a straight A student, so I had to compensate for receiving Bs on my report cards. Before I returned the signed packet to my teacher, I would put all the papers back together and re-staple them as if my grandma had seen every assignment I did.

One of my grandma's daughters lived near our house—"across yonder," we would say—but within walking distance. She was my favorite aunt of them all. She and my Uncle Bubba would glorify my honor roll status. Uncle Bubba would always say, "Come on here Essence, let us see what an honor roll report card look like!"

Boy, the glare and teeth-sucking Aster would give from hearing that. She was always telling me I was not that smart and nobody cared about my honor roll report card. Apparently they did, and she did not like it. One time in fifth grade, I received a C on my report card in science and my Aunt Zira could have burned that school down. She was not having it. I did not receive Cs on my report card so the teacher must have made a mistake—not I who did the work but the teacher. The next day, Aunt Zira was at that elementary school telling Mrs. Porter how she must have given me the wrong grade because I do not make Cs. I know Mrs. Porter probably thought she was crazy. However, she nicely told my aunt that I had received the grade from the work that I submitted. Basically, I submitted C work. I made sure to not receive another C the rest of that school year.

I loved my Aunt Zira. She was more of a mother figure than anything. I was also a hustler and I knew I could hustle a couple of dollars from her if I worked for it. I would clean her room, vacuum her living room, wash her dishes, and just about anything else she needed me to do for a couple of dollars. I even used to clip her toenails. I did not mind cutting her toenails, but those things would be curled over her toes; if I was not careful, one might have tried to fly into my eye. Actually, I think one did. I just wiped my face, kept on cutting, and polished those toenails right on up. One toenail was not going to stop me from getting paid. It was not so much about doing the work or the money; it was the time and attention I received being at her house. She showed me the love and attention that I longed for from my own mother. My Aunt Zira taught me how to cook, and to this day I still love to cook, especially macaroni and cheese. She was the best auntie any girl could ask for. She loved me and I could feel it.

Aster was never one to show any type of affection or love. I was a touchy-feely type of person. I loved to hug. I hugged everybody. Aster made it quite obvious that I was not to hug or show her any type of affection. I lived with a complete stranger.

We would have to catch our school bus the second go around. This meant we had to make sure we saw the bus drive down the road and it would pick us up after it turned around. One morning, I missed seeing the bus go down the road, so I believed that it had not come yet. As I walked past the dining room window, I saw Aster standing at the end of our driveway. I thought to myself, *Ole heifer must have seen the bus go down the road and was not going to tell me.* Our driveway was pretty long compared to my little legs, so she must have been standing there for a while. Well, at least I know she did not just walk outside. I scurried trying to get my coat and book bag so I would not miss the school bus. Missing the school bus was the worst thing ever at Grandma's house. She made it very clear that she was not going to be too happy if she had to take one of us to school. As I ran down the side stairs, I missed the last step and fell on my ankle. It was the worst pain ever. I looked up to see if Aster would at least come help me. Of course, she did not. She turned around and smirked as I lay there trying to get up. I hopped all the way to the end of our driveway, thinking of every curse word I could say to her when I got close enough. I stood there silently. I was afraid. I have always been afraid of my sisters. They were bigger than me, so that meant they were stronger than me, right? At least that is what I always believed. Any time they said or did something hurtful towards me, I would just take it. I thought there was nothing I could do to defend myself. If their words hurt as badly as they did, just imagine their hands.

This was one of the many times I wished that Mommy was decent enough to raise me. She was gone, so there was no more that she could do to defend me. I wanted her protection but I also did not want to be afraid anymore. Grandma would take up for me and tell them to leave me alone whenever they were mean, but sometimes I did not like for her to do that. Her defense just made them meaner. I thought with Iris gone, dealing with one of them would not be so bad. Boy, was I wrong! Aster had enough anger to equal to a thousand people. She never had a problem reminding me that I was black and ugly. Black and ugly. Black and ugly. Black and ugly. I heard it so much that I started believing that only the pretty kids were the light-skinned ones. I wanted to be lighter skinned so badly. Then I could be pretty. As crazy as it may sound, I wanted to be just like Aster. As mean and hateful as she was, she was who I chose to be inspired by. She had no emotions and nothing hurt her. She was stone cold and heartless. At least that is how I perceived her to be. Everything hurt my feelings, even down to the smallest thing and I hated how sensitive I was. Why would I not want to know how to not be emotional all the time?

Aster could not love me but she, just like I, had never been loved or taught to love ourselves or others. I felt us to be so different, but years later I would realize we were about the same.

FOUR

Summertime and holidays as a kid were lit! We spent summertime traveling the east coast visiting family. For the holidays, most of the time family would come to Grandma's house. It was even more exciting spending time with my cousins. My grandma's sons (my uncles) would take us to the lake and we had cookouts. I loved the love. I loved the attention. The majority of the tim, Aster did not have time to even notice I existed and that was the best feeling in the world. My grandma's children were very family-oriented and there were not too many events that we did not attend. I felt extra spoiled by all of my aunts and uncles. If I was not receiving gifts, I knew I was going to be taken shopping or receive money.

Going up north was the best. I loved New York and everything about it. New York people have a different style and demeanor. They seemed fearless. I enjoyed spending time with my oldest sister as well. Because she did not live in the house with us anymore, she seemed to be nicer to me. I hated when summertime was over. Even though I enjoyed going to school, life felt like it went back to normal. I was starting to hate my normal life. I liked being around happy people and not restricted to animosity and anger all of the time. I would cry whenever it was time to return home or family would leave Grandma's house.

I was excited about going to the sixth grade. All the different elementary schools were combining and there would be new faces to make friends with. I was excited that I tried out for the cheerleading squad and made it. I was mostly shocked but very excited. The summer before sixth grade, I attended a summer camp in the next county over. The camp was at Ocheke College. There were kids from all the surrounding counties there and that summer I met my best friend.

I loved going to the swimming pool. A bunch of females would get dressed in the bathrooms and these girls did not care who they took their clothes off in front of. I would try to get a stall but there were so many girls in there that usually all of the stalls would be taken by the time I got inside. One particular day as I was undressing and putting on my bathing suit, I saw a girl who clearly did not know how to properly wear her bathing suit.

"You know you got to take your underwear off before you put on your bathing suit, right?" I obviously did not know how to mind my business but I thought maybe she did not know her underwear was still on and showing through her bathing suit. Crazy right! How could she not know when she put it on?

"Yeah, I know," she said, obviously embarrassed by the fact that I drew attention to what she was trying to keep hidden.

Not minding my business actually made me a friend. We both attended different elementary schools. That is why I never saw her before. In sixth grade, all of that changed when the schools merged.

Mara Lewis was her name. I may not have remembered her name but when I saw her on the first day of school I definitely did not forget her face. She had not forgotten mine either. There were two sides to sixth grade. The best way I could remember it was having two sides of the hall. The kids in my homeroom class were the kids I saw in just about all of my classes besides electives. Mara and I were not in the same classes together but we still found ways to communicate. We would write each other letters telling each other about ourselves. In the evenings after school, we would talk on the phone until one of us was told to get off. Mara lived with her grandmother too. Her grandmother was her mother's mom and they were originally from the Bronx, New York. We would often joke about which borough was better, Queens or the Bronx. I told all about my family and how I came to live in Virginia. She knew how much I despised my sisters for always being mean to me for no reason. She had an older sister who was above herself as well. She had much insecurity about herself, which I thought was crazy because in my eyes she was perfect. One of her insecurities was about her weight. When they say opposites attract, they really do. As much as she hated being as big as she was (which was not that big), I hated being as skinny as I was. I wanted to be her size so badly. I used to force myself to eat as much meat as I could at dinnertime trying to gain weight. If I was bigger, I would look more intimidating and would not be picked on.

We could relate on so many levels. She became the big sister I always wanted. During the weekends, I always begged Grandma to let me stay at her house. Mara's grandma was nothing like mine. Sometimes my grandma did not want me to stay over at friends' houses. She would tell me I had a home, so why not let my friends come stay with me sometimes? I did not want my friends staying with me often though. Even though I told them about Aster, I did not want them witnessing how mean she was to me. I was actually embarrassed by how afraid I was of Aster. I would talk a lot of shit about her, none of which I was brave enough to say to her face. From what I told my friends, they were not too eager to meet her. Aster did not care who she embarrassed me in front of and she especially liked to do it in front of people I really liked or who liked me. I think she wanted them to see how much of a punk I was. I would not have admitted it then, but I really was a punk and very afraid of her. I never stood up for myself for fear of what she might do. I just let her do and say whatever she wanted to me, and when I had time alone I would just cry. Such a punk!

I really wanted all of my friends to like me and I would have done anything to get their approval. I could not show them how afraid I really was because I believed they would not want to be friends with such a scared person. I always ran to someone to defend me in situations where I did not want to defend myself so it was easier to deal with conflict. I just did not deal with my own conflict at all. I knew how to curse though. My way of hurting people was with words. I could break a spirit with the nasty words that would come out of my mouth, but I was very sensitive to the things that people said about or to me. It does not really make sense now that I think about it. I could dish it out but I damn sure could not take it back in.

My best friend was everything to me. Every time she would stay at my house, I would let her sleep in my bed and sometimes I would sleep on the floor. My grandma did not like this because she felt that it was my bed, and I should not have chosen to sleep on the floor to accommodate someone else. I would cook her breakfast food sometimes and my grandma always felt like I did entirely too much for my friends. What Grandma did not understand was that I had always wanted a friend who could be more like a sister to me, someone I could laugh with and tell all my secrets and desires to without the fear of judgment or ridicule. I had never experienced that type of love until that point in my life, and I was willing to do anything to make my best friend want to remain in my life for the rest of my life. Aster did not like the relationship I had with my best friend. I did not quite understand why though. For years, I tried to get Aster to bond with me or spend time with me and it was never something she wanted to do. God forbid someone should show me some attention and actually like me. I was at the place in my life where I stopped caring how Aster felt. I always cared more about her feelings than my own. This time she was not going to run off the best person I had in my life.

CHAPTER FIVE

Aster got pregnant when I was in seventh grade. I was so excited to be an auntie. I worried tremendously about my nephew's life. She and Ahadi, my nephew's father, would fight like cats and dogs—well, correction—she would mostly fight him from what I could see. I liked Ahadi; he was nice to me. One time, he was at Grandma's house and Ahadi and my sister were in her bedroom. Next thing I knew, they were coming up the hall arguing and fighting. Aster obviously did not care that she was pregnant. Ahadi never hit her, but in that moment I wished that he did. As he was walking—obviously walking away from her—she was jumping and smacking him on his head. His head just kept hitting the wall and I was anticipating the backhand he never gave her. I wanted him to smack her all the way back to the bedroom. I liked when people stood up to her because they had the balls to do what I could not. If he would have bopped her in her head a few good times, I would have pretended as if I had not seen anything. I may have even shaken his hand, but I guess his balls were as small as mine that day. Well no, he is a man and men do not hit women, but that day could have been an exception. Not too long after that incident, my nephew was born earlier than expected. Not too long after he was born, Ahadi committed suicide at the Ronald McDonald house, which is a home where parents can stay when they have a sick child in the hospital.

My favorite cousin in the whole entire world was Nala. She was my Aunt Zira and Uncle Bubba's daughter. Just about everywhere she went, I would be right there with her. We would spend time cooking each other breakfast in the afternoon, going to the mall, and hanging out at her boyfriend's family home.

Aster did not like the relationship Nala and I had, and it showed. Every time she referred to Nala, she called her my sister, saying, "My sister Nala—she is your sister not me." That did not bother me one bit. Little did Aster know I really wished Nala was my actual sister, and in my mind, she was. Even more so, I loved that Nala was black like me, and she was pretty. If she could be pretty and black, I could too. So yes, Nala was my pretty black sister.

One time when I was in eighth grade, I told Grandma I needed to ride with Nala on a school trip to help her with something. I do not remember the lie I came up with but Grandma wrote the note for me to be able to leave school early. All day, I waited for the sound of the intercom from the office informing my teacher I had permission to leave. I sat in tech class with my books ready because there was no need for me to get started on an assignment. By the time they called me to the office, I was already at the door. I did not even wait for the hall pass. That day, we rode to the mall so she could get her boyfriend Scar some shoes. He was not the nicest person in the world but was pretty comical at times. His aunt and uncle would get drunk and put on a show. His uncle was tall and once those drinks kicked in, he would stand on this small table dancing and singing. Scar's aunt would fuss for his uncle to get off the table but he did not pay her any mind. I enjoyed watching drunken people cut up. That small living room at Scar's aunt's house would be filled with the smell of liquor, cigarettes, and sweaty drunk people. I wanted to be there to see it. My clothes would smell so heavily with cigarettes that when I got home I would have to get naked at the side door and throw my clothes in the washing machine. Grandma neither smoked nor liked the smell of cigarettes, so I was not about to walk past her room smelling like them. I was afraid if she smelled me, she would not let me hang out with Nala anymore.

My grandma and my Aunt Zira had a strong dislike for Scar. One reason was he was older than Nala—much older. I think that was also their reasons number two, three, and four not to like him as well. In their eyes, he was a thug and Nala was too good to be with him. Well, she was, but as long as she was happy, I was happy for her.

I believe in my entire life there was only one time Nala made me mad. One night, I had gone with her to Scar's aunt and uncle's house like usual. Scar's aunt and uncle had moved to a slightly bigger house just down the street from their old one. I was in the house on the phone with my then boyfriend Kion as Nala, Scar, and his aunt and uncle were outside on the porch. I never saw Nala drink but Scar did and at times he would become a bit much with the words that came out of his mouth. This particular night, as I sat in the house on the phone, Scar came in the house drunk, asking me who I was on the phone with. He kept saying, "It better not be no boy, you better not be on the phone with no boy!" Well I was, and did not feel the need to tell him I was because it was my phone. He then sat beside me and kept asking for my phone but I was trying to hurry and get off the phone so he would not take it. That was when he put his hand over my knee and squeezed so deeply a sharp pain ran through my body. I screamed for him to get off me while watching the door to see if Nala was going to come in the house but she never did. I did the only thing I could think to do at the time. I sunk my teeth as deep as I could into his arm and I bit with every ounce of life I had left in me.

He jumped back so fast but he damn sure let my knee go. I sat there as he yelled, "You fucking bit me! This bitch bit me!" He ran outside where his aunt, uncle, and Nala were still sitting on the porch telling them I bit him.

His aunt came in the house, saying repeatedly, "You turned Scar red, black, and blue! You turned Scar red, black, and blue!" In my mind, I was thinking, *So no one heard me yelling for this nigga to get off of me, but now it is a problem because he is red, black, and blue?* He would have bruised easily anyway. He was damn near white his complexion was so light. All I know is he never touched me again, but that is only where the night began.

Riding in the back of the car on the way home, I got back on the phone with my boyfriend and Scar was hysterically drunk and mad. He was yelling profoundly as I was telling my boyfriend at the time what had happened. Nala never really said anything but an occasional, "Okay Scar, all right." I was thinking, *Is that all she is really going to say?* Scar started telling me how he would take my phone once again. I tried to ignore him and kept trying to talk and stay on the phone until I got home. As I previously stated, he was mad and drunk and did not like the fact I was ignoring him. Before I knew it, he turned around, reached to the back, and smacked that phone right off the side of my face. I was pissed. How dare this nigga think he could take my shit that does not belong to him? I kept yelling for Nala to make him give me my phone back. She would tell him to but that was not enough for me. I wanted her to take my phone from him. I got so mad in that back seat I started shaking.

It was about two o'clock in the morning and I was about to raise some hell. I knew my Aunt Zira despised Scar and I was about to wake her up and tell her what he did. Nala had an older sister named Dahlia who was at the house at the time, which I did not know. I do not even think Nala had put the car in park before I jumped out of it and ran to the door, banging on it for dear life. I was about to wake my auntie up and she was not going to like this. Nala ran behind me with the phone, but by that time I did not care about that phone; I was telling. Dahlia came to the door and I spilled everything that had just happened. If I did not know anything else at that moment, I knew Dahlia was going to get that phone back. Nala finally caught up with me and gave me my phone back, but I was pissed with her. She not only let this nigga hurt me, but did not defend me against her drunken boyfriend like I thought she should have. I walked home in the dark. I may not have gotten to Aunt Zira, but I would wait until Grandma woke up in the morning. She was going to get the both of them. That was not the end of Scar's rampage that weekend.

Lily was visiting from North Carolina that weekend, and the day before the incident with Scar occurred, she and I did something a bit mischievous. I never snuck out the house before, but I think Lily did it on the regular. I was scared but she was brave. That night, she wanted to go chill with my neighbor. The neighbor's house was not far, but it was far enough for me not to want to walk to it. I was so scared, it was dark, and there were dogs outside. Oh yeah, and Spider from the previous chapter was this neighbor's dog. I believe by this time Spider had died, but there were still strays that I was not about to be running from in the dark on my little legs. At the same time, I could not let Lily walk by herself. I kept asking her over and over again what we were going to be doing when we got there. She said they were going to smoke some weed, talk, and chill. I asked her again. I think the more innocent it seemed, the more I could build up the courage to go. One thing was for certain: I could not let her walk up there by herself in the dark.

Finally, the fear died down a bit, but I told her we could not go out the front door. I refused to walk past Grandma's room in the middle of the night and have her catch us. We went out the window. We headed up the street and arrived at the house. As they chilled, I got on his computer to change my Myspace layout. I did not smoke nor drink so I had to find something to entertain me as they did. When we got back to my house, the chair we used was folded up on the side of the house. Lily and I began questioning if we had put the chair on the side of the house or not. We could not remember so we climbed through the window and went to sleep.

Come Sunday, Lily and I went to church just like any Sunday. After church, Nala came to Grandma's house to tell Grandma she was going back home to Robeson, North Carolina. Scar never really spoke to Grandma because Grandma did not like him either. That Sunday, he came in the house with Nala, which I found to be odd. I stayed in my room. I did not want to see or speak to either of them. Did I mention I never told Grandma what happened that night Scar was drunk? I just let it go. I listened through the door to hear what he was saying. This no good yellow nigga was telling Grandma how the other night I had snuck out of the house. Apparently Nala and Scar had driven past Grandma's house that night and saw the chair in front of my window. He put the chair on the side of the house so I would not get in trouble. He was dry snitching because I bit him, which I was well in my right to. I ran up that hallway so fast. Nala looked very ditsy in the face. I could not believe she was going to let this nigga snitch on me and she knew he was in the wrong. I had something for his ass.

"Nuuuhhuuh—no, no, no, no no. He is lying, Grandma. He only mad because I bit him the other night when he squeezed my knee. Then he snatched my phone out of my hand while it was on my face. Yup, smacked me right up side my head. And I bit him. I turned him black, red, purple blue. I bit him hard because I told him to let me go and he would not. He was drunk and Nala did not do anything. She let him hurt me." Boy, was I singing. Oh, he thought he was about to tell something. He really thought he was about to get me in trouble? Me? He had the game all messed up. Grandma forgot all about the chair and sneaking out of the house. This yellow negro put his hands on Essence and that was all she heard. It is fair to say I did not get in trouble but Scar did. As they left, I stood behind Grandma with my arms folded, because you cannot get one up on me.

SIX

My Aunt Zira and my Uncle Bubba were two of my favorite people in the whole world. They were like the parents I had wished to have. As stated before, my Aunt Zira taught me how to cook and turned me into a little hustler early on in life. My Uncle Bubba taught me how to drive, first with the lawn mower then with a car. They would take me to college football games, which were very exciting for me. I did not know much about football but enjoyed being able to get out of the house. I often rode with my Aunt Zira after church because I knew she was going to Walmart and I was going to be able to get whatever I wanted. My Aunt Zira took up for me quite often as well. When I did not want to deal with my middle sister and her attitude, I would go to my auntie's house.

My grandma had this thing about tearing up her property. I made sure to put things back how I found them and where I got them from. One of Grandma's pet peeves was the vacuum cleaner cord. We had to make sure to wrap it back up once we were done and I never forgot. One, I went in grandma's room to get the vacuum to clean my floor. The vacuum cleaner cord was laying beside the vacuum. All I knew was I did not leave it like that. I did not pay attention to the cord and just picked it up and took it into my room. As I plugged in the vacuum, I noticed the cord was stripped and the wire was showing. I did not want to use the vacuum with the cord like that. I told my grandma and even showed her the cord. I told her how I found it, not accusing anyone of anything except in my mind. Aster began yelling how she did not mess up the vacuum cleaner cord and I must have done it. I attempted to explain calmly once again how I found the cord and that I had not used the vacuum yet. She kept yelling and insisting I stripped the cord. At that moment, I was just trying to make sure I did not receive a whooping for something I know I did not do. I refused to use the vacuum and put it back in Grandma's room with the cord wrapped around it like it was supposed to have been.

I sat on my bed while Aster kept ranting on and on. I was going to ignore her because as long as I knew in my mind what I did and did not do, that was good enough for me. To give you a perfect visual of how this next scene played out, I am going to describe how my bed was made. My bed was actually a bunk bed, but the top mattress and the board holding the mattress were missing. The only piece there at the time was the frame of the bed and of course my bed at the bottom. As I was sitting on my bed, Aster ran into my room, jumped through the bars, and began choking me. I had never once defended myself against her and was shocked by her entering my room. I slid all the way to the wall and off the bed with her hand on my neck. I never thought to block the hits, only to get her hands from around my neck. I began scratching at her hands and trying to dig my nails as deep as I could. We managed to get off the floor but she was still choking and hitting me. I had a long body mirror on the adjacent wall. She slammed me up against that mirror, shattering it, then she let go. My grandma was a few steps away sitting at the dining room table; she did not budge. I rubbed the back of my head and neck to make sure no glass had entered, then I put my shoes on and left. I ran, actually, afraid that she would come outside and chase me down.

As I crossed the ditch, I noticed that my Aunt Zira was not home. I kept running to this lady named Marigold's house. That was not the first time I ran to Marigold's house, so I am sure she already knew who it was when I came knocking. I told her everything that had happened and how I did not want to go back to Grandma's house. Grandma ended up her calling her and told her I better get home soon to clean up that glass off my floor. I could not believe that I was being left to clean the glass up when it would not have been there if Aster did not do what she did. As I got older, that is how most of the confrontations at Grandma's house went. She went from defending me to ignoring the things my middle sister would do and say. I guess Grandma thought I should be able to defend myself but I did not know how. I never really had to with more than words and I was scared. Aster was bigger—much bigger—and I did neither liked nor wanted to fight. I never did at that point. I preferred to be left alone; it made more sense not to associate with someone you did not like.

I began hating them both, my Grandma and Aster, at this point. Aster would try to fight Grandma all the time, and I am talking in her face fistfight type of fighting. Grandma mostly shooed her away, never really getting as physical with Aster as she did me. I got my ass tore out of the frame. I think she even killed me one time and brought me back to life. It did not matter to Grandma if I hit the floor, fell over into a box of toys, or was lifeless; she kept swinging. If the end of the belt did not hit a desired location on my body, it hit everywhere. A few times, she tied me up to the bathroom cabinets. One day, either she did not tie me tight enough or my wrist was too small, and I was able to slide my hands out of the loops without breaking them. I made sure they lay perfectly against the cabinets then I crawled into the tub and lay there. My grandma wore these loud flip flops and before she came back I could hear her. I jumped out of the tub, slid my hands back to through the loops, and hung my head. I assumed that the purpose of tying me up was so I would be worn out. I tried to look as worn as worn could look so I could come out of the bathroom.

Now I am not going to lie: I do believe in not sparing the rod because it will spoil the child, but I think Grandma missed the whole point. I do not think the scripture meant take that rod and beat the life out of the child. She literally did not want anything left of you when she beat you. I was terrified of that one but I dared not speak up or talk back and I damn sure would not fight back or resist punishment. I am not going to say Aster was never punished or to the extent that I was, but I never saw it or cannot remember it. Grandma was so stern that one time she beat me before we went to church—while we were in the parking lot. Could you imagine having to not only go into church after being beaten but being a part of the guest choir? I was in that church hoping Jesus was going to strike her down, sinning and then singing his praises like nothing ever happened. To make it worse, I was in the front row trying my best not to burst out in tears. My throat was dry and I knew if I opened my mouth, I was going to cry the loudest cry. I knew she could not whoop me in that choir, but I had to go home with this lady.

SEVEN

Music was always my escape. I loved all types of R&B music. My favorite artist was Mary J. Blige. At my young age, I may not have experienced all the things she or any other artist expressed through their songs, but it was the pain for me. Something about when Mary sang, I could feel the pain she was feeling through her voice. I felt her pain so deeply I would cry about her adversaries. Whenever I was upset or sad, I would lock myself in my room, turn on some R&B music really loud, and drown out my thoughts through the sound of the music.

One summer, my grandma, Apollo (my adopted father), and I went to New York. We were going to visit family as usual. Apollo had this old, long car which he worked on constantly. He was so cheap, instead of getting someone to fix the car when something broke, he would attempt to fix it himself. You see I said attempt, right? That summer, after his failed attempt at fixing the air conditioning, we had to ride eight hours in the scorching heat. To make matters worse, I, not thinking apparently, decided I wanted to wear an orange jumpsuit. I really believe that was the moment I stopped liking to wear the whole jumpsuit. Now I will wear either the jacket or the pants but never the two together. I thought I was going to die in the backseat of that car. The closer we got to the city, the more traffic was backed up, so for period of times we were just sitting there and I was roasting.

That was the same summer after Aster had my nephew early. I do not remember all the details about the fight between her and Grandma, but when we returned from New York she had moved out all of her belongings and I was glad.

My Aunt Zira made it very clear with her constant criticisms that she did not like Apollo. Apollo was technically her stepdaddy because he had married her mom, but even to this day, she will not call him Daddy. I sometimes joke with her about it and she reminds me that he was my daddy because I had his last name. Well, I do, but to me that did not mean anything. I only had this last name to be able to move to Kentucky. They did have to adopt me, which I later on in life found out Apollo did not want to do.

If I am telling it right, my grandma met Apollo through my biological grandmother (my mom's mom). They were all friends, so I assume that is how Apollo and my adopted grandma met. My biological grandmother had lung cancer and probably knew she was going to die, so she asked my adopted grandma to take in my sisters and me if she passed. My biological grandmother was in the process of adopting us herself when she passed away. She must have known her daughter (my mom would never get off of drugs or be stable enough to care for children. My biological grandmother also wanted to keep my sisters and me together.

Grandma and Apollo argued a lot. When he was nice, he was Grandpa, and when he was mean to Grandma, he was Apollo. They liked to drink. I am not quite sure if most of the disagreements they had were while they were intoxicated, but I just know they drank very often. As a child, I learned to stay in a child's place, but I was nosy and would at times try to ear hustle to know what they were arguing about. No matter what it was, Apollo would disappear for a period of time and then he would come back as if nothing had ever happened—at least until the next argument broke out. I knew they were good when I would get of the school bus and he was on the back porch shelling fish. Every single time this man came back, he brought fish. I used to believe that fish made the old people calm and love each other more because this man's return with fish never failed.

Apollo was bald and skinny and my grandma was more on the hefty side. He had this knot in the front of the middle of his head. I always wanted to know how it got there and why it never went away. One day I asked him how the big knot got on the front of his head and he told me to ask my grandma. I skipped my nosy tale self right on in that kitchen where Grandma was at the time.

"Grandma, how did Grandpa get that big knot on the front of his head?" I asked.

"Go ask him," she replied, not giving me the answer I was looking for.

"But he told me to ask you." I reversed the question right back on her.

"Well, he kept bothering me one day and so I took a cast iron pan and bust him in the head," she stated with this big smile on her face.

I backed up, turned around, and looked at Apollo as he nodded in agreement. I remember thinking *Oh, so you just go around fuckin everybody up, huh?* I knew better than to say it out loud, but one thing was for certain: if you messed with Grandma, she did not mind fighting you.

When I got a little older, I asked Nala why Grandma's children did not like Apollo. It was mostly my Aunt Zira who I heard express a strong dislike for him, but I was being nosy. I wanted to know. She told me that Apollo did not want my grandma to adopt my sisters and me. One summer, we went to New York and when we came back, Apollo had removed everything from my grandma's house. When I say everything, I mean the stove, refrigerator, kitchen tables, couches, beds, televisions, and just about everything else my grandma owned besides our clothes. My grandma's children had to help her replace everything in her house. That sounded like a good enough reason to not like someone to me. I just did not understand why, if he did all of that, she kept taking him back. That incident had to have happened when I was between three and four years old because I do not remember it. However, I do remember seeing Apollo living at our house for quite a while, sleeping in the bed with Grandma, and all of that. No matter what he did or said, she took him back. Sometimes I would hear her on the phone asking him to come home and leaving him voicemails when he did not answer. I did not understand why she thought she needed him so badly.

EIGHT

Many things occurred in my life the summer after my seventh grade year. I was only thirteen years old. I was just a little girl. My life changed so drastically that I felt like someone had pulled a rug from under my feet and I landed on my ass very, very hard.

At that time, Nala was still kind of living with her parents and we still hung out from time to time. One particular summer day, I woke up and probably did not even wash my face or brush my teeth before throwing on some shoes to run to my Aunt Zira's house. I wanted to hang out with Nala that day and I had to catch her before she left home to go anywhere. It would have made more sense to have called her, but that is not what I did. I did not even put on decent clothes. I just walked over there in sneakers and my nightgown. We were all family anyway, right?

I got to my auntie's house and Nala and Scar were walking from her room. I spoke to them and asked her she was about to do. I believe they were going out of town but wherever they were going, I could not go and Nala told me she would see me when she got back. Okay cool, I would just head home. I stood in the kitchen watching Nala and Scar leave. As I turned to walk out of the door, my Uncle Bubba called me into his bedroom. I did not think anything of it at the time. I figured he was going to ask me to do something for him before I went home. When I entered the room, he was lying under a blanket and the television was on. He asked me did I know what he was watching on the TV. I turned around and looked at the TV. It was a man and a woman having sex. I felt stuck, like this was a trick question. Was he trying to figure out if I was having sexual intercourse? I was confused so I told him no, I did not know what exactly it was I was supposed to say. He told me to sit down in the chair beside his bed so I did.

Then he pulled his blanket back and asked me did I know what he was holding in his hand. That was the first time in my life I had ever seen an actual penis. I sat there, still confused about what he was trying to get me to say. He asked me if I liked the way it looked and I just shrugged my shoulders. He talked to me about my breasts, which I barely had, and about my vagina. Then he asked to see my vagina. He told me it was okay, that he would not touch me and only wanted to see. I opened my legs while sitting in the chair. My uncle had this smirk on his face and made a sound of satisfaction. He asked me if I could take my underwear off and I did. He told me how pretty my vagina was and to never shave it as he started stroking his penis. He told me to touch my vagina so I put my hand on it and he instructed me to rub it up and down. I did everything he asked. He stroked his penis until he ejaculated. Even after the semen came out, he still kept rubbing and asked me did I like it. I sat there staring at him, not knowing what to say.

Afterwards, he wiped himself off and I pulled my panties back up. He offered me some money and told me this had to be our secret. If I did what he asked, he would give me money but my grandma and Aunt Zira could not find out. I got up from that chair and when I hit the door, I ran. I ran as fast as I could. I do not know why I ran so fast because he was not chasing me, but the only thing on my mind at that time was calling Mara. I ran into the house and Grandma was sitting at the dining room table by the door. I asked her if I could use the phone right quick. By that time, we had a cordless phone so I could take it into my room. I dialed 6-3-5-2-7-8-2. The anticipation as the phone rang made it feel like the phone was ringing for hours. As soon as her grandma answered the phone, I asked to speak to Mara. When she got on the phone, I told her everything besides the part of what I did. I just told her what he asked me and about watching the sex scenes on TV. I was so embarrassed. I could not tell her that at times I fondled myself in front of my uncle. What would she think of me? I do not know what she would have thought but his asking was bad enough and Mara was going to protect me as she always did.

My Uncle Bubba never physically touched me, but he would often make me masturbate for him. Sometimes we were in his bedroom, my cousin's room after she moved out, and even the living room. He liked pouring baby oil on my vagina as I rubbed it and at times would get me to rub my breasts as he masturbated until he ejaculated. Then he would give me money. Sometimes he would call Grandma and tell her to send me to the house when my Aunt Zira was at work. I would tell Grandma I did not want to go, but in the minds of the adults around me, when they told you to do something you had better do it. I would ask my uncle at times why he always wanted to see my body when he had my aunt. He told me that my body looked nothing like hers. I was young. I was constantly reminded by him how what was happening was all right because I was not biological family and was not really his niece. I always looked up to this man as a father figure and he did not even consider me to be his niece.

Sitting in my room, I would hear my grandma on the phone telling everyone who would listen how great her son-in-law Bubba was and it used to make me sick. At that time, the only person who knew what was going on was my best friend Mara. Eventually I told her grandma, but they never told. I felt nasty and so shamed that I could not just say no. I did not have to go back each time. I could have simply run away but I had nowhere to run. We lived in the country—like the *country* country. In my mind, if he could offer me money to see my body then the money belonged to me, so I started stealing it. The perfect time to steal from my uncle was when my aunt was home. I used to wonder if he knew I was stealing his money because he always had big amounts of cash in his wallet. Whatever he had the most of I took the most of. If it was a lot of twenties, I would take more of them. I did not just stop there. I checked the tens and the fives too.

It was easy to steal it too. I would tell my Aunt Zira I needed a pad or some soap from her bathroom as they sat on the couch. He was not going to follow me when she was there and I knew he kept his wallet on the nightstand beside the bed. I would shut the door just enough so it was not all the way closed or suspicious. I took the wallet into the bathroom, racked up, and grabbed a pad or bar of soap so it looked like I got what I came for. Then I went home. One time I even stole one of his sex videotapes. I took some of the film out of it and shoved it back in the cassette player. I was mad, angry, and ashamed. He took something away from me and I was going to take anything and everything I could get my hands on from him, and I wanted his money.

I used my uncle to take Mara with me to football games when school started. He would always ask me if she had money before she was picked up, and I would lie and say yeah. Then when we got to the gate, he would pay. During the games, I would go back and forth in the stands asking him for money so Mara and I could get snacks and food. I hated him and I wanted nothing more than for him to go broke.

At one of those football games, I saw the first boy I was ever to have sex with, Rudo. He was a high school student and I was only in the eighth grade. I did not care. I thought he was cute and he looked just like Chris Brown (well, back then he did). I wanted him to be my boyfriend. I do not quite remember how we started actually talking to each other but we did and I liked him a lot. I even thought I loved him. I realize that back then I loved everybody who was nice to me. A month before I turned fourteen, I snuck him into my house while Grandma was at church and I lost my virginity to him. The crazy thing was I had to pay his ride gas money for him to get there. (He still owes me my ten dollars). Of course, I called Mara and told her I had sex. I literally told this girl every single detail about my day and my life. If I woke up and caught a cramp in my toe, Mara knew it.

The relationship with Rudo did not last long. Towards the end of my eighth grade year, he started ignoring me and not returning my calls. He got a job at Wendy's, so I just chalked it up to him being busy with school and work. I got a little attention here and there from him and a few gifts.

That summer, I went to New York to stay with my Aunt Violet. My Aunt Violet is my Aunt Rose's daughter. She and my Uncle Aslan had a nice apartment in Rochdale. They were both New York City police officers, so they were very strict even down to the food I ate. I enjoyed going there though because my Aunt Violet always made sure I enjoyed myself and at times I did not want to leave. I got a job at MS42, a middle school where they were doing a summer camp for kids. It was within walking distance from my aunt's apartment so it was convenient and I was able to mingle with people my age.

One weekend while my aunt was in her back room sewing, I was watching music videos in the living room. I got hungry so I went in the kitchen to find something to make a sandwich. I made two sandwiches and then my phone rang. Before I could eat, I checked my phone and it was Wendell. I got excited and answered. I had not spoken with him in a while.

"Hello!"

"Hey, what's up? What are you doing?"

"Nothing much. Just made something to eat. What about you?"

"Nothing. Chilling. Aye look, I got to tell you something."

"Okay, I am listening."

"I got this new chick I am fuckin with and she got big titties and she thick."

He continued to ramble on and on about this girl he met while working at Wendy's. My heart dropped into my chest and eventually we just got off the phone. I put my plate of food in the refrigerator and went back into the living room. As I sat down, the next music video to come on was "Say Goodbye" by Chris Brown. What an oxymoron! I was so heartbroken.

When that Monday came, I dropped the shirts and jewelry he had given me in the incinerator on my way to work and did not think any more about him the rest of the summer.

NINE

Aster ended up moving back in to Grandma's house for a while. She was still hateful as hell, but I did not have to engage with her much. I had a little more freedom with staying over at friends' houses. One day, she asked me to ride with her to the store; that was odd, but I went. Once we got a couple of miles up the road, she asked me something that I did not want to talk to her about. I did not want to lie either, so I told a partial truth.

"Has Uncle Bubba ever touched you or did anything inappropriate with you?" she asked.

"Um, like why would you ask that?"

Now I was about to sweat bullets in my seat. I hated being put on the spot.

"Because he always buying you stuff and taking you places. Every time he calls the house, he calls specifically for you. Just seemed suspicious," she said, never taking her eyes off the road.

"Well yeah, well I mean he never touched me or anything. He just asked—"

"Asked? Asked you what Essence?" she demanded.

"You know, to see my body and stuff."

I could not tell her that Uncle Bubba had me masturbating in front of him. That would be too embarrassing, and by the tone of her voice, she was upset. Might I add this was the first, last, and only time in my whole life that Aster had considered how I felt in a matter and showed any type of concern for me.

When we got back to the house, she told Grandma about Uncle Bubba asking to see my body. My grandma asked me why had I not told her before, and I told her I was scared. She called my Uncle Bubba and Aunt Zira and asked them to come over to the house when my uncle got home from work. My Aunt Zira did not come.

By this time, my Aunt Violet had been called and told about what was going on, and she was highly upset. She suggested calling the law, which never happened. My grandma asked my uncle why was he asking to see my body parts and he stated that he was only joking. Aster was yelling and cursing at him, calling him all types of names. Iris, who was still located in New York, was called as well. Then Uncle Bubba had the nerve to ask me about his tape in front of Grandma. He asked me if I took the film out of one of his porn movies. He had already questioned his nephew about it. I lied and told him that I did not. I did not care about him mentioning his porn movie as long as he did not mention his money being stolen. Either he did not notice or he figured I did not tell everything that was going on so he was not going to either. My grandma looked at me and said, "Well, he was joking but I do not see what part of the joke she found to be funny." The whole situation was brushed under the rug and everybody went on about their lives like nothing ever occurred.

The women in my life were not good examples of how to be treated by a man. I did not know how to have love and respect for my body. I would have done anything for that daddy love, even if it meant being persuaded to do things that were wrong to get it. If I knew then what I know now…

My Aunt Zira rarely spoke to me again after that. She would speak, but it was obvious that things were different. I did not go to her house for a long while and did not sit beside her at church. There were times when she would not even look at me. I could feel the tension but I did not understand why her tension was directed at me. Because she distanced herself from me, I was glad I did not tell everything that had happened. I refused to tell Nala. I could not lose her too. When small conversations did occur between my Aunt Zira and me, they felt very awkward. There were times when I would ask her to do something for me, or anything of that nature, and she never failed to mention that she was not my mother. I never thought she was my mother, and I never called her Mom, Mommy, or Ma. She was a mother figure, but I knew exactly who she was in my life.

Grandma was never Momma to me; she was simply just a grandma. Aunt Zira was a version of Momma I wished I had. When she discarded me from her life, it felt as if I had lost a mother twice. She would often remind me that I was not her child and would go period of times without even speaking to me. I lost a biological mother and a mother figure, and it burned in my soul to know that I was never good enough for either one to love me. Why was loving me so wrong?

Most of the whoopings I got when I was younger were because I would lie about things not to get in trouble. I would act up in elementary school and try to forge my grandma's signature on the slip so she would not find out. The teachers knew it was not my grandma's signature and would make me call her to tell her what I did. As soon as I got home, I would get the black beat off my ass. Whenever I acted up at home, sucked my teeth, walked too hard when I walked away from Grandma, or anything else she found the be disrespectful, I was beaten. She always said if I told the truth, my whoopings would not have been that bad. Yes, I was a liar. I lied to keep from getting into even more trouble, which always got me into even more trouble. What little kid does not tell lies? The one time I told a partial truth made me public enemy number one. How could you raise a child to be honest yet be angry at the child for being honest? I always believed that Aunt Zira just did not want to be known as the one with the defective husband. At least that is what I told myself to rationalize her new nonchalant behavior. I was also a kid—a very tomboyish kid at that. However, none of that mattered. Things were different and if my aunt ever wanted me to feel unwelcomed, she did a damn good job. Mara's grandma believed me. Eventually I told her but I could not stay at their house all the time. I just wanted to go somewhere and never come back.

TEN

I bought all my school clothes for the ninth grade and no one ever questioned where I got the money. I was excited and nervous about going to high school. Rudo was a twelfth grader when I was in ninth grade, and I made up my mind that I would not associate with him. I ended up meeting someone new anyway. His name was Kion. His grandma lived right up the street from my house. We ended up dating and I fell in love instantly. He was tall and dark-skinned, and one of the sweetest boys I ever met. He was also very manner able. There were times when he would walk from his grandma's house to my house at night, and of course we were having sex. I would sneak him in through the window. After a while, he complained of the far walk, which was pretty far to be walking, especially in the middle of the night, so I gave him my bicycle. I told him everything about my life up until that point, and he and Mara became my confidants.

I met my friend named Azalea in the sixth grade when I was cheerleading. We ended up reconnecting once I entered high school. For a while, I was hearing how a girl named Zinnia did not like me. At the time, I did not even know who she was until one day someone pointed her out to me in the hallway. Even after seeing her face, I could not figure out why she expressed a strong dislike for me. Any and every one I knew who had a class with her would tell me how she would talk bad about me the whole block. I was at my aunt's house one day on the computer modifying my Myspace page. I came across a picture of Azalea and Zinnia on Azalea's page. I told Azalea she looked cute and questioned why she was in a picture with Akon's little sister. The next week at school, my comment under the photo was the talk. Apparently, Zinnia did not like the comment I made, as she should have not, and was telling people she was going to fight me. I had not heard the insinuation of the fight until the day of.

It was Wednesday so I had my JROTC uniform on. We were inspected for wearing our uniforms properly on Wednesdays. I went to my first and second block class as usual. While in second block, a girl named Camellia came up to me right before the bell rang and told me that Zinnia would be waiting for me by my locker before lunch with a lock to fight. I thanked her but I never thought more about it. No one who had previously expressed this girl's dislike for me had said anything about a fight the entire morning. I believed it was just hearsay. I turned the corner of the front hall to head to my locker. There, a big swarm of people blocked my way and in the front was Zinnia. I have had a few scuffles here and there but I had never really had an all-out fight. I did not know what to do. I walked down the hall, threw down my books, and we began fighting. Luckily the lock must have swung out of her hand because I never remembered being hit by it. The fight was broken up and we were each escorted to the office. I did not win, by the way. I had a little scratch on my forehead, but I do not remember hitting or punching her back. To be honest, I did not know what I was doing.

Once I got into the office and was instructed to sit down, I started to replay the incident in my head. The fight was not the most devastating part; it was the people standing behind her who knew the fight was going to happen. The main person I could remember seeing was Kion. He not only beat me to my locker but was standing on her side. This meant he knew what was going to happen. and others who I thought did friend whom would tell me about her not like me. They were all and plus more were standing behind her. My thoughts were interrupted once I heard Mara's voice. She was running up and down the hall past the office asking where I was. She had A lunch so she was in the cafeteria when everything occurred. I was suspended for ten days and I was furious.

Grandma came to the school to pick me up and on the ride home I just knew I was going to get my ass whooped when we got there. She asked me what had happened. I told her about the accusations beforehand and everything that happened after and up until that point. She said okay and went into the house. She did not say anything else about it. I could not let it go because I was embarrassed. Zinnia did not like me. I did not even know her! I had to sit at home for ten days because she had no self-control. Well, neither did I. I changed my clothes and walked right over to my aunt's house. Now that I think about it, I should have taken a nap or something, but I wanted to get right back on Myspace. I went to that same picture and told Zinnia that when I returned to school I was going to stab her. I do not remember if I deleted it before or after I got caught, but eventually I did delete it. Zinnia never responded, but I know for fact she saw my comment.

My ten days at home fell around spring break so I ended up being out of school an extra week with everybody else. During that time, my grandma went to Panama and would still be in Panama when I returned to school, so I stayed at Mara's house. The Sunday before I was to return to school, we were watching *College Hill* and that season they were in the Virgin Islands. I do not remember the girls' names but I know one got mad at the other, took the heel of a stiletto, and bashed into the other girl's face. That is what I wanted to do to Zinnia. I even practiced hiding a box cutter in my bra. By the time I returned to school, I did not want to stab Zinnia anymore. I just wanted her to leave me alone. I saw her that morning before walking into the school. Her bus was parked right beside Mara's car, but I never spoke to her. Mara and I walked to my locker and she walked with me to my first block, which was gym.

It was a regular day. No one mentioned anything about the fight or the threat so I hoped it had been forgotten. After gym, I gathered my bag and headed toward the main building. As I was walking, I saw Jack Zona, the principal, and Mrs. Clover, the assistant principal, and an instant feeling of anxiety shot through my body. Now what the hell could they want? I just knew they were coming for me and I was not wrong. Mrs. Clover escorted me into the girl's locker room and asked me where the blade was as she searched my body. The first place she went was my breast but nothing was there. She took the soles out of my boots and emptied my book bag while inquiring about the blade or knife. I kept trying to tell her I did not have one. They then escorted me to the office. This time I was not suspended; I was being expelled from school and charged with a crime. I tried to explain to them that my guardian was out of the country, but apparently they did not leave me until after constant calls to my house with no answer. I did not have a phone number for my grandma, and even if I did, she was not going to jump straight onto a plane and come right away. They called Mara's grandma and let her come pick me up from school. I was pissed off. If I wanted to stab Zinnia, I would have done so when we saw each other getting off the bus, but she reported the threat to the office. I went to Mara's house and waited for Mara to get home from school. I stayed off the internet too.

When Grandma returned, Mara's grandma explained to her what happened. She was not upset about the incident. Nothing could be done at the time besides go through with the court appearance and go in front of the school board. Grandma put me in summer school to get my English credit. The next school year, I was sent to a Christian academy.

ELEVEN

I returned to Wikalo High School my eleventh grade year. By that time, a lot of things were different. Mara had made a new best friend, Lilac, and she was acting differently from when I left. Kion and I were still supposed to be dating, but I found out he was having sex with other girls who lived on his road. He had moved to his mother's house on Betco Road, not too long after he got caught sneaking into my house one night.

I had a job at a fast food restaurant and obtained my driver's license a little after returning to public school. I probably had the most friends and hung out with people I never had before once I was able to drive. I learned early that as long as people saw you as a benefit, they would consider you a friend. I still desired to be liked by others, so I often gave rides to people just for company.

One night I got my grandma's car stuck in Kion's mom's yard and, while spinning the tires, red mud splattered all over the car. To make matters worse, he and his cousin Ralph had a puppy, which I had in the back of the car, and it left a smell. The next day, Grandma was pissed about the red mud and the car stinking, so she told me to wash it. I pulled the car to the front of the house, and when I was done, I attempted to back the car to the side of the house. While the car was in reverse, I went to tap the brake but mashed the gas, and backed the car into our shed, knocking it off the foundation and cracking the car's bumper. Grandma was mad and I was mad—and I do not even know why I was mad, to be honest.

For a while, Grandma stopped letting me drive her car to work. I started catching rides with my cousin Daffodil, who worked at the same establishment. The job was decent at first, until one day Daffodil got into a heated argument with a manager and walked out. I was stuck trying to figure out how I was going to get home. A girl named Yasmin offered me a ride home.

Rides home turned into chilling with Yasmin, her sister Marguerite, and another coworker Leilani after work. They were all older than I was, and not in high school. They would have kickbacks at Leilani's house and this is when I first started drinking. I would give them the money and they would buy whatever drink I wanted. I started off drinking grape Joose. I did not need a whole can because it did not take much for me to get drunk, but I would usually down the whole can. There was an incident one night when I was so drunk that I went in the house and lay down. Leilani had a cousin named Thorn and I had called him to ask if I could lie in his bed while he was not there. He told me yes as long as I did not throw up in his bed. I went and lay down. A little while later, I heard Leilani, Marguerite, and Yasmin calling my name. I could not move. I knew if I got up, everything inside of me was coming out. They came into Thorn's room and told me to come out of his room. In my mind, I told them Thorn said it was okay for me to lie in his bed but I do not think the words actually came out of my mouth. They lifted me up on both sides and I threw up all over myself and Thorn's bed. They threw me in the shower and turned the water on. That was the first time I ever had no control over my body. I really thought I was going to die that night.

Mara had moved to New Jersey, but returned not long after twelfth grade began. We did speak to each other every now and then while she was in Jersey, but she was nothing like the person I had known before. Kion and I had an on again, off again type of relationship. I had come to accept the fact he was never going to be faithful to just me, so I stopped being faithful to just him.

I missed a lot of days during my twelfth grade year to the point I almost did not graduate. The school year went well until second semester. Kion was expelled for fighting. I skipped a lot of days to be with him. I started smoking weed and drinking much more heavily than before. He had this idea of being a rapper and had no real life goals. I had a lot of faith in him but I had also become accustomed to the attention I was receiving from other males.

Mara began hanging out with Kion's sister Sage a lot. I thought their friendship was rather strange, but if she liked it, I loved it. I called Mara's house one day and her grandma told me that she was at Kion's house. I did not think anything of it because she was friends with his sister, but I feel like I missed exactly what her grandma was trying to tell me. It was snowing outside, so I had to shovel a path around my car to get it out. While driving to Kion's house, I came around a curb and my car slid down a small hill. The fire department was called by a person who seen the incident. The fire chief told me, after pulling my car back into the road, to go home. Of course, I did not listen and continued to Kion's house. Mara was there but it did not seem like she was there for Sage. I told Kion about what happened with the car but I could tell he was more irritated at the fact that I was there. I started talking to Mara, and Kion went walking up the road. I felt in my heart that something was not right about the situation but I ignored my intuition. They were just friends, I told myself, but deep down I did not believe that to be true.

Over the next months, I did anything and everything I could to rekindle the relationship with Kion, but it was over and I could not accept the fact. I could not believe that it was over at the hands of my best friend. I always had that intuition that something was not right in their friendship. Even though he had been expelled from school, he stated one day that he was going to take Mara to our senior prom. Another day I was on the way to school and Mara's house was on the way to the school. I had this feeling that Kion was at her house, so I turned around and went to her house to see. Mara came to the door; I asked her if he was in there and then he appeared. The night before, I had tattooed his name across my chest and I went to my best friend's house to show him what I had done. I felt like such a dummy but he still kept implying that they were just friends.

Mara and I continued to pretend to be friends and I tried to accept her relationship with Kion. I still told myself it was just a friendship and that I was tripping to assume anything else. We all were smoking and drinking together. We began stealing Triple C (coricidin) from any store we could. One night, I lay in his bed while they were on the porch smoking and I felt so left out and embarrassed. I wanted to be high too. Maybe then I would fit in with them. I took a pack of Triple C, which was eight pills. I sat there for a while and did not feel any effects from it. I grabbed another pack and took eight more; still nothing happened. I lay down, and after some time passed, I woke up. I was so high I could barely hold my head up. Mara and Kion were sitting in the living room huddled up on one couch and all I could do was sit there and stare at them. I began itching profusely and believing bugs were crawling on me. There were a lot of roaches in his house, but in my mind they were on me. I scratched the bend in my arm so badly it began to bleed.

Not too long after this incident, my grandma went to Panama and asked Kion's mom if I could stay at their house while she was gone. She took my house key because she did not want me bringing anyone into her house while she was gone. Kion's mom left about a week after to go to New York for a funeral, leaving him and Sage in charge of their younger siblings and younger cousin. One night Mara and I went into Walmart to steal. We would have gotten away with it but as we walked out the lawn and garden door, we were stopped by an undercover shopper. As we sat in the security room, there was a moment when we were left alone. I took some of the stuff Mara had and hid it behind some boxes beside me. She was already eighteen and I was seventeen, so I could be charged as a minor and have the charge expunged from my record.

The officer entered the room and asked us both what our names were. I told the officer my name was Essence Jones. He left the room, I guess to check our names. He came back into the room and asked me again what my name was. I told him Essence Malone. The officer immediately told them to lock me up for using aliases. Mara began yelling "no" and "why" and threw her hand in front of me as if that would have stopped them from taking me if they wanted to. I told the officer that my name was Essence Jones Malone, which was true. I was more upset at the fact we had been caught than worried about the officer doing his job. As we waited for Mara's grandma to come, my phone kept ringing. Mara asked the female officer if I could answer my phone because something had to be wrong, and she stated that I could.

Two of Kion's friends were at the house with him. They were calling me to come pick them up because they had to go home. They stated that something was wrong with Kion. He was walking around the house in a ski mask and sweating while listening to one song by Lil' Wayne over and over. I explained to them that I had been caught stealing from Walmart and could not leave but would get there as soon as I could. Because my grandma was out of the country, the officers let me leave with Aster, who was working at Walmart at the time, as long as she followed me to Kion house. Mara's grandma came to get her. En route to Kion's house, my middle sister was pulled over so I continued on without her.

When I got to Kion's house, I tried to talk to him but he was obviously out of his mind. It was winter, but he was practically naked. I took the boys home and headed to Mara's house to tell her about what was going on. Mara and I went to the hospital where Lilac was having her first child. We sat outside for a while smoking weed after the visit and I came up with the idea that maybe Kion would talk to Mara instead of me.

When we got to Kion's house, he was fully naked except for a ski mask, blasting Lil' Wayne, and sweating. He looked scary and I had never seen him like that before. He went in the bathroom, took dish soap, and began wiping it under his arm in an aggressive manner. Sage told Kion to put some clothes on because Mara was there and he made the statement that it was not like she had never seen him naked before. Sage looked on in disbelief, Mara looked shame-faced, and I looked stupid. It is one thing when you know something and act on it. My intuition had been right, but I had not trusted myself enough to act on it, which was really embarrassing. I took Mara home and went back to Kion's house. I did not want to, but I had nowhere else to stay and I was beyond exhausted.

I knocked on the door several times. At first, I thought I was going to have to sleep in my car. Eventually, Kion came to the door, still naked with the ski mask on, peeking around the door as if he did not want to let me in. I told him I was not going to bother him and I was just going to go to sleep. He let me in. I went to his bedroom, shut the door, and lay down to go to sleep. Not too long after that, he swung he door open and told me not to shut any doors in his house. The music was blaring, he was rapping repeatedly, and I was becoming afraid. I lay down and attempted to go to sleep. I dozed off pretty fast but was awakened by pressure at my feet. As I was coming out of my sleep, I caught Kion about to hit me in the face with a Bible. I yelled at him and asked what was he doing as he hit me up and down my body with this Bible. He stated that he was going to get the devil out of me. The boy was clearly possessed. I sat up in bed and begged him to get out of the room, which he did. I tried my hardest to stay awake, dozing here and there.

The next morning, the kids were running around the house. Nobody was really getting ready for school and Kion was still in his possessed façade. I started fussing at Kion for not getting the kids ready for school and to cut out whatever mess he was on. He and Sage began to argue before he stated he was going to steal some money out of my car. I chased him and once I was outside, he threw my keys in the snow. I searched for my keys until I found them but could not get back in the house. He had locked the storm door. He went back on attack with Sage as I pulled and yanked to get the door open. Sage finally got out of his grasp and opened the door for me. Kion and I began to argue because, at that point, I had no clue as to what he was on or doing. Then he threw me on the couch, got on top of me, and hit me straight on the nose with the palm of his hand. I was choking him by his Bart Simpson chain, trying to get him off of me.

I suddenly felt a fluid running out of my nose so I turned my head to the side to see blood drop onto the floor. Kion instantly jumped up as I ran to the bathroom to discover my nose bleeding. Sage and the other kids, beside the youngest sister who was not in school at the time, had eventually left the house on the way to school. I called Kion's Uncle Carnation to come to the house to watch him as I packed my stuff up to leave. The only other place I could go was to Mara's house until my grandma came home. I was just too afraid to turn my back on him or leave out of the house without all of my belongings in case he locked the door. Carnation arrived but did not really want to intervene. I told him I just needed him to stand there to make sure Kion did not follow me into the room. Carnation ended up going home, so I called Aster as Kion called his mom. Aster could hear the derogatory remarks Kion was yelling in the background and instructed me to call the police then call her back. I did. While I was on the phone with Aster, Kion was telling his mom I broke up things in her house and made a mess. His little sister kept asking him for juice; I would have poured it for her but I did not want to leave the front door. She kept saying to Kion "juice, juice," but he continued to ignore her while talking to his mom. His little sister then went to the refrigerator and grabbed a container of juice and brought it to him. While trying to pass him the container of juice, some of it spilled into his lap and he told his mother I poured juice all over him. Aster asked me where was I in the house and I told her I was still standing at the door. I also told her I did not pour juice on him; his sister did accidentally.

The police finally showed up and asked what was going on. One officer was talking to Kion; I pulled the other officer aside and told him something was not right with Kion. I told the officer I did not mind leaving the house; I just wanted someone to watch my back as I took my stuff out of the house. The officers informed Kion that they did not have to make me leave because he told them previously that I lived there.

An incident had occurred right before his mother left for New York. Kion had hit the speed limit sign not too far from his house. Because he did not have a license, he sped home, ran into the house, and told me to tell the police that I was driving the car. I had just gotten out of the shower when they arrived, so the police officers knew he was lying. At that point, Kion told them I was living at that address. Had they had checked my driver's license, they would have seen that was not true. On the day of his outburst, the same officers came to his house. By that time, I was exhausted, so I packed my stuff and went to Mara's house, where I her grandma everything that had happened.

Later that night, I received a call from Sage. She said Kion was still acting crazy, and had taken his little sister, who was wearing only a diaper and a t-shirt, walking up the street. He was holding her in the air. Their cousins from North Carolina had stopped by the house and could not calm him down. Mara and I drove to Kion's while her grandma called the police to tell them they needed to return to his house. I parked my car in a cut not far from his house, and Mara and I walked up the street. I tried to stay in the shadows of the trees so the street light would not hit me as Mara walked ahead of me. Kion came to the road before I could make it closer to the house. He took one look down the street, as if he could smell me, and started chasing me. I made it to my car in time. I drove to pick up Mara and his siblings. As I did, I saw him in the road hitting his sister with a tennis racket. I had never before in my life seen such a possessed person.

Once everyone was in the car, I headed to Frankfort, Kentucky until a police officer called my phone instructing me to come back. While standing outside talking to a police officer, Kion became irate and began disrespecting his father and another officer on the scene. They attempted to put him into the back of a squad car, but he soon kicked car window out so they called for a van. Kion was tased several times, but it did not faze him. Once the van arrived, several officers tried to put him inside. Kion, however, put his head and on top of the van to prevent them from forcing him inside. An officer asked what was he on and I told him I did not know. I had been trying to tell people, his father included, that something was wrong with him. However, no one listened to or believed me.

TWELVE

Months after the incidents with Kion, I found out that his weed had been laced by one of his friends. This was the same friend who set him up to be jumped at his house. I had told him this person was not his friend.

I neither loved nor respected myself, so I attracted people who did not love or respect me either. I taught people how to treat me. I must admit I did not treat myself well—the others just followed suit.

I got high and drank just about every day. Kion was sent to several pavilions; that limited our contact until there was no contact. I became much more promiscuous than I was in high school—looking for love in all the wrong places.

I tried to go to the military after high school but was unable to pass the hearing test to get into to the army. I have been unable to hear in my right ear my whole life. I continued working at a fast food restaurant and I continued to drink. I drank so much. I would do anything to numb what I chose to ignore inside.

On Thanksgiving morning in 2010, I received my first DUI. I did not go to jail, but it cost a lot of time and money to get my license back. I was embarrassed to be the youngest person in an alcohol safety program. To me, I did not have a problem; I just got caught.

Over the next ten years, I had failed relationship after failed relationship and also bore three children. I believed that having children would bring me happiness. I forced myself into people's lives, trying to prove to others that I was worthy and deserved to be loved. My friendships were just as bad as my relationships. I was constantly arguing and fighting with people who I should have had let go. I held on to some people for too long. I needed people to understand me and appreciate the sacrifices I made to enhance relations that had already expired.

Alcohol made me numb and accepted my excuses for being the way that I was. I could not let go of the pain. The pain defined me so much it was how I introduced myself to others. I just wanted to be loved. My children have seen me in hostile situations and relationships with men that showed them I had no self-respect or sense of self-worth. The pain turned into anger that I became unable to control. I have made bad choices and poor decisions in search of a love that I should have been looking for within. I have spent the last thirty years trying to find my purpose in the world. There is no possible way to replace the love I did not receive as a child, and I carry the burden of that pain. It felt like a mold that grows and grows; each time I shaved a layer off, I added more mold until it became unbearable. People always said I played a victim, and I did, but all I knew was how to wallow in self-pity.

One of the worst places to be at war is within your own mind. Having good memories is great, but what memory refuses to forget is haunting. One thing I learned while learning to love myself is not to expect more from people. Some people really give all they have and sometimes all they have is just a little bit. Whether it is a little bit of love, time, or affection, people give you the most of the little they have. I know that there are others in the world who may not have been shown how to love another person adequately. I have not learned that either, but I am learning that I reflect the type of attention I attract. Because I had no self-respect, it was easier for others to disrespect me. It is almost unfair to require others to treat me in a way that I was not willing to treat myself. I am learning to forgive not only others but myself. I self-sabotaged a lot of situations. They say if you know better you do better, but at the time I did not know any better.

As a child, I never understood why Jesus asked his Father to forgive those who had harmed Him. He stated they did not know what they did. I often expected people to know the pain they had caused me and know how I felt. However, it was unfair to ask them to understand when I was causing the majority of my pain by not letting those people go. To ask for understanding of my circumstances, I learned I must also be understanding of others and use better discernment in who deserves to be in my life. Jesus knew that Judas would betray him and He still allowed Judas to sit at His table. Jesus needed Judas. Jesus knew He had to die so our sins could be forgiven, and He needed Judas to do what he did so that it could come to pass. No one ever wants to deal with the pain of betrayal and heartbreak, but it is often in our weaknesses where we find our strengths. The pain I endured was intended to help me grow and to learn to make wiser decisions from my own bad examples.

My healing has made my future seem so much brighter, once I learned to move from the other side of the sun.

I apologize to anyone I may have harmed while trying to figure out my own life. I can admit that I was not always in the right. I take full accountability for my words and actions. I wish you all the best with love.

To my children,

First, I would like to start by telling you how much I love and appreciate you. I admire your strength and your ability to fight through every obstacle that you have faced. I apologize for not giving you the respect you deserve. I did not see your worth or value. I apologize for making the wrong choices and decisions that have put you all in compromising situations. I wanted to have children to make me happy and that was very selfish of me. It is not your job to make me happy. It was my job to learn how to make myself happy so I could better guide you through your own lives.

You all have experienced the unhealed version of me. I was a scared little girl who knew nothing about being my own person or being a mother. I did not know how to teach you to love yourselves because I never knew how to love myself. I know I do not deserve to have such wonderful children as you, which makes the guilt of not being the best mother for you unbearable at times. I pray that God keeps me here long enough to see you all grow to be old. I pray for guidance to better assist you all in your lives. All of you mean the world to me and are my greatest blessings. I would give anything to go back and raise you in a better way. I thank God for second chances and opportunities. I am going to work hard to give you all the life you deserve.

I never want you to feel as if you are not loved by me because I love you with all my heart. Mommy just had to learn how to love herself first. It is impossible to pour into someone else when my cup is empty. Now I am filling my cup with all the positive and loving things

I need to properly love and guide you. Mommy is not perfect, but I try. Until my last dying breath, I will love you, and after I will love you in spirit.

Always,
Mommy

ABOUT THE AUTHOR

Dolly Baker was born in Queens, New York. She was later relocated to South Hill, Virginia, in August of 1995, through the foster care system. As a single mother of three, Baker strives to influence others by her life story and her journey to self-love.

Printed in the United States
by Baker & Taylor Publisher Services